Contents

What is a garden?

A garden is a **plot** of soil.

People grow plants in a garden.

Material Detectives: Soil

Let's Look at a Garden

Angela Royston

www.raintreepublishers.co.uk
Visit our website to find out more information about **Raintree** books.

To order:
 Phone 44 (0) 1865 888112
 Send a fax to 44 (0) 1865 314091
Visit the Raintree Bookshop at **www.raintreepublishers.co.uk** to browse our catalogue and order online.

First published in Great Britain by Raintree, Halley Court, Jordan Hill, Oxford OX2 8EJ, part of Harcourt Education.
Raintree is a registered trademark of Harcourt Education Ltd.

Editorial: Andrew Farrow and Sarah Chappelow
Design: Jo Malivoire and AMR
Picture Research: Erica Newbery
Production: Duncan Gilbert

Originated by Modern Age
Printed and bound in China by South China Printing Company

10 digit ISBN 1 844 43636 5 (hardback)
13 digit ISBN 978 1 844 43636 1 (hardback)
10 09 08 07 06
10 9 8 7 6 5 4 3 2 1

10 digit ISBN 1 844 43641 1 (paperback)
13 digit ISBN 978 1 844 43641 5 (paperback)
11 10 09 08 07
10 9 8 7 6 5 4 3 2 1

British Library Cataloguing in Publication Data
Royston, Angela
Soil: lets look at a garden – (Material Detectives)
620.1'91
A full catalogue record for this book is available from the British Library

Acknowledgements
The publishers would like to thank the following for permission to reproduce photographs:
Corbis p. 6; Digital Vision p. 19 (tiger); Ernie James/NHPA p. 8; George W Miller/Science Photo Library p. 5; Getty Images/Photodisc p. 19 (earthworm and fish); Harcourt Education pp. 14, 17, 22 (sand and soil), 23 (crack), 24; Holt Studios International 2003 p. 12; Holt Studios p. 21; Oxford Scientific p. 20; Paul Hobson/Alamy pp. backcover (mole), 18, 23 (tunnel); Photodisc pp. 4, 23 (plot); Photolibrary/Eric Kamp pp. backcover (boots), 13; Tudor Photography/Harcourt Education Ltd pp. 7, 9, 10, 11, 15, 16, 22 (concrete), 23 (concrete, crumbly, and wilting).

Cover photograph of flowers reproduced with permission of Flowerphotos.com

Some words are shown in bold, **like this**. You can find them in the glossary on page 23.

Soil holds the plants in place in the garden.

What is soil?

Soil is a layer of earth.

Plants and some animals live in soil.

Soil feels **crumbly**.

It can make your hands dirty!

Why do plants need soil?

Soil gives plants water and food.

Most of the water comes from rain.

This soil is too dry and the plant is **wilting**.

What should you do?

You should pour more water onto the soil!

The plant takes in the water.

The plant soon begins to grow again.

What kinds of soil are there?

Some soil is very sandy and dry.

It blows around in the wind.

Some soil is wet and muddy.

It sticks to your boots!

Where do flowers grow best?

Flowers grow well in soil that is not too sandy or too wet.

Can you grow a flower on **concrete**?

No, you cannot grow a flower
on **concrete**!

The flower would die.

Some plants grow in the **cracks** in concrete.

They grow in the soil between the cracks.

What animals live in the soil?

Moles live in the soil.

They dig **tunnels** to move around.

tiger

earthworm

fish

Which of these animals do you think lives in soil?

Earthworms live in the soil.

They eat fallen leaves.

Earthworms break up the soil.

They make it easier for plants to grow.

Quiz

Where do plants grow best?

Look for the answer on page 24.

sand

dark, **crumbly** soil

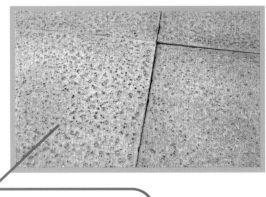

concrete

Glossary

concrete
material that looks like stone. It is made from a mixture of sand, gravel, cement, and water

crack
small gap

crumbly
breaks up easily

plot
marked out area

tunnel
hole underground

wilting
slowly drying up and falling over

Index

Answer to quiz question on page 22

A plant would grow best in the dark, crumbly soil because it is not too wet or too dry.

Note to parents and teachers

Reading for information is an important part of a child's literacy development. Learning begins with a question about something. Help children think of themselves as investigators and researchers by encouraging their questions about the world around them. Each chapter in this book begins with a question. Read the question together. Look at the pictures. Talk about what you think the answer might be. Then read the text to find out if your predictions were correct. Think of other questions you could ask about the topic, and discuss where you might find the answers. Assist children in using the picture glossary and the index to practice new vocabulary and research skills.